Everything i Know i Learned On Acid

Coco Pekelis

Acid Test
Productions

◁ DEDICATION ▷

For Toby Dalton, my wild knowing boy,

who connjures the universe according to his own design

≺ ACKNOWLEDGMENTS ≻

Where We Give Credit Where Credit Is Due

All praises to my husband, David Dalton, whose addled vision is to blame for this book. Any complaints should be addressed to him. My undying gratitude to Stacy Kreutzmann Quinn, who was foolhardy enough to embark on a book with an author whose philosophy of life is procrastination, rationalization and the avoidance of responsibility. Many thanks to my editor, Nancy Reid, who pulled it all into focus, and my agent, Franki Secunda, who moves in mysterious ways.

A tip of the hat to Art Spiegelman and Bob Schneider, whose *Whole Grains* blazed the trail.

And finally my Trophy of the Unknown Freak Award to Paul Krassner for keeping alive the flame of inspired lunacy with his *Confessions of a Raving Unconfined Nut*.

Book design: Noren Schmitt, Magma Design,
62 Forbes Avenue, San Rafael, California 94901
415.455.9092

The art that appears in this book includes a self-portrait drawing copyright 1996
by Coco Pekelis. All other art culled from the following titles published by
Dover Pulications, Inc., New York:

African Designs from Traditional Sources, copyright 1971
The Complete Nonsense of Edward Lear, copyright 1951
Fantastic Illustrations of Grandville, copyright 1974
Posada's Popular Mexican prints, copyright 1972
Fanciful Victorian Initials, copyright 1984
Withchcraft, Magic & Alchemy, copyright 1971
North American Indian Designs, copyright 1993
Southwestern Indian Designs, copyright 1992
Northwest Coast Indian Designs, copyright 1994
Egyptian Designs, copyright 1993
Celtic and Early Medieval Designs from Britain, copyright 1983
Treasury of Fantastic and Mythological Creatures, copyright 1981
Authentic Indian Designs, copyright 1975
Hand Shadows, copyright 1967
Outlines of Chinese Symbolism and Art Motives by C.A.S. Williams, copyright 1976
Alice in Wonderland Coloring Book Pictures by Sir John Tenniel, copyright 1972
Old-Time Advertising Cuts and Typography, copyright 1989

Acid Test Productions
2447 Petaluma Boulevard North
Petaluma, California 94952
707.769.7484
Fax: 707.765.6018
AcidTest@ix.netcom.com

Printed in Hong Kong

‹ TABLE OF CONTENTS ›

SELF PORTRAIT CONTEMPLATING THE INTRODUCTION BEFORE ARISING

< INTRODUCTION >

What I Did in My Life by Coco Pekelis

I have not only taken the sayings in this book to heart, dear Reader, I have lived them! I hold advanced degrees in the art of dropping out. Forget be here now—be here next has always been my motto. ❦ Today was the latest in a long string of days I'd set aside to write this introduction. I'd planned to get up early, as I always do (plan to, that is), but things conspired against me right from the start. Upon awakening I found one of my favorite cats asleep on my foot, and if there's one thing I will not do, it's disturb a cat. Actually, that's one of many things I will not do (more of that anon). ❦ Let's see, where was I? Oh yes, trying to get on with my day. I think. Anyway, it must have been almost noon by the time I got downstairs and rustled up a pencil and paper. Unfortunately I make it a point never to write on an empty stomach. Too desperate. So I fixed myself some eggs and was going to have a cup of very strong coffee but I couldn't find where I'd put the damn stuff and it occurred to me that if I'd rearrange my shelves _alphabetically_ these things wouldn't happen. I could just run my fingers along the jars of anchovies, apricots, almond butter, Bosco and baking powder until — _voila!_ — coffee! On the other hand, _now_ was probably not the time to begin anything (it never is) so I made a note to consider, at some future time, the rearranging of my shelves. ❦ My desultory habits were formed, for better or worse, many years ago. Perhaps a brief account of my life in the sixties might help to explain how I came to my philosophy of life, such as it is. A few weeks after receiving a Master's Degree in something-or-other I ran away to join the circus, and let's just say it's been gloriously downhill ever since. With the Bread & Puppet Theatre, I traipsed across the country in a painted school bus. I wandered the globe with Meredith Monk's notoriously avant garde dance company (featuring absolutely _no_ dancing). I worked in a Stonecrete Buddha factory, sold _Divine Toad Sweat_ on the corner of St. Mark's Place and Second Avenue and painted black-light seascapes for Taiwanese hippies. I was a pole-raiser for the Tamalpais Tepee Construction Company, and sang in a dive _across_ from Madison Square Garden. I've been a Kirilian photographer, a den leader for the Boy Scouts of America, and a tour guide for Atlantis, Mu and beyond. I've rescued animals who didn't want to be rescued and looked up strange facts for strange people. 🐈 Alas, dear Reader, all this procrastination and rationalization has not made my life an uneventful one. On the contrary, there is nothing like dropping out for embroiling one in misadventures. There's the time Bob Dylan thought my purse was a waste paper basket. And the time I ended up with the Grateful Dead on stage at Woodstock because a security guard mistook me for Mountain Girl. 🐈 I've had plenty of opportunities to make something of myself, but have refused on the grounds that it might lead to steady employment, a split-level in the suburbs, Barcaloungers and the Republican Party. I even turned down a career in the music business when the Eleventh Floor Elevator Operators asked me to be their road manager. Fine, I said, as long as I don't have to go on the <u>road</u> (or leave my room). And I met Don Juan <u>way</u> before Carlos Castenada. I flew across the Yucatán with him (and I don't mean in an airplane). The old codger begged me to write his autobiography, and I <u>wanted</u> to write it, I <u>intended</u> to write it, but, well, you know . . . the cats, the coffee, the kitchen shelves. 🐈 I was tear gassed at Fort Dix and

Chicago, but slept through Altamont and the levitation of the Pentagon. I always devour the Sarah Lawrence alumnae notes but have never contributed to them. I have squandered my days sipping cappuccino and perusing my to-do list. I <u>think</u> of everything, but that's as far as it goes. Like Proust, I'm an old tea-head of Time and horizontal scribbler. If I were a blonde I'd be a big, lazy blonde reading movie magazines and eating bon-bons. 🐛 Oh, yeah, the introduction. Well, it's not cancer research, now is it? I mean it's only a book, right? And it isn't as if I haven't made a start. I'll call Stacy, my publisher. She'll understand.

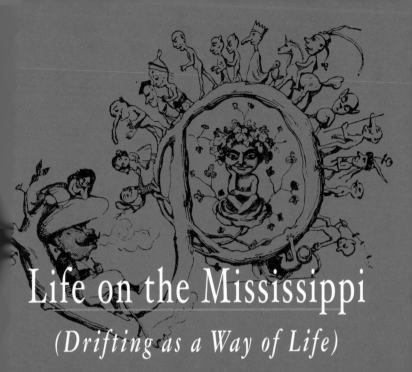

Life on the Mississippi

(Drifting as a Way of Life)

drifting: n. to move from place to place without regular employment and with no particular goal.

Mississippi: home of mojo, the blues (see below), grits, open tuning, the bo weevil and Bo Diddley.

the blues: pl. n. almost always has 12 bars.

live oak: n. (1) moss covered Southern tree, purported entrance to the underworld, viz: Virgil, Dante, Tennessee Williams etc.; (2) one of the things you might come across while drifting — along with the Midnight Special, Jack of Diamonds, Route 66, pay phones, former lives, dime stores & bus stations, the teachings of Don Juan and matchbooks with phone numbers on them.

I Quit!

Taylor Mead

It was kind of solemn, drifting down the big, still river, laying on our backs looking up at the stars . . . We had mighty good weather as a general thing, and nothing ever happened to us at all.

Mark Twain,
The Adventures of Huckleberry Finn

It takes a lot of time to be a genius. You have to sit around doing nothing, really doing nothing.

Gertrude Stein

Lord, this is an huge rayn!
This were a weder for to slepen inne!

Chaucer,
Troilus and Criseyde, c. 1385

Action is the last resource of those who do
not know how to dream.

Oscar Wilde

Scribble thoughts flowing freely from the
mind, sing in good voice, keep the beat and,
above all, accept a glass of wine when it is
pressed upon you.

Yoshida Kenko, *Essay in Idleness*, 1340

Every decision you make is a mistake.

Edward Dahlberg

Destroy yourself physically and morally and
insist that all true brothers do likewise as
an expression of unity.

Robert Hunter,
The Ten Commandments of Rock

Good swimmers are oftenest drowned.

Thomas Fuller,
Gnomologia, 1732

Every hero becomes a bore at last.

Ralph Waldo Emerson

The sole cause of man's unhappiness is that he does not know how to stay quietly in his own room.

Blaise Pascal, *Pensées*

Show me a hero and I will show you a tragedy.

F. Scott Fitzgerald

We don't need no stinkin' badges.

Treasure of the Sierra Madre

Oh well, no matter what happens there's always death.

Napoleon

Nobody ever did anything very foolish except from some strong principle.

Lord Melbourne, 1779-1848

Good resolutions are useless attempts to interfere with scientific laws.

Oscar Wilde,
The Picture of Dorian Gray

Give me chastity and abstinence, O Lord, but not today.

St. Augustine,
Confessions, 397-401

It is better to waste one's youth, than to do nothing with it at all.

Georges Courteline, 1917

I have had a good many more uplifting thoughts, creative and expansive visions while soaking in comfortable baths in well-equipped American bathrooms than I have ever had in any cathedral.

Edmund Wilson

I never indulge in rhyme or stanza
Unless I'm in bed with the influenza.

> **Quintus Ennius,**
> **239-169 BC**

So long as a man rides his Hobby-Horse
peaceably along the King's highway, and
neither compels you or me to get up behind
him — pray, Sir, what have either you or I to
do with it?

> **Laurence Sterne,**
> ***Tristram Shandy***

Pleasure is the beginning and end of living happily.

Epicurus, 341-270 BC

The best way to fill time is to waste it.

Marguerite Duras

I too for years past have been stirred by the sight of a solitary cloud drifting with the wind to ceaseless thoughts of roaming.

Matsuo Basho,
The Narrow Road of Oku, 1680

Let's dig one o' those little greasy truck stops . . . I'd like ta talk with those truck drivers 'n' hear what they gotta say about life on the road. Yeah . . . I bet they got wild stories of the road. Drivers . . . Trucks . . . Hijackers . . . Fights! Yeah!

R. Crumb, *Fritz the Cat*

The Eskimo, Ootah, had his own explanation. "The devil is asleep or having trouble with his wife, or we should never have come back so easily."

Robert Edwin Peary,
The North Pole

't know what street

Canada is on.

Al Capone

There are moments when everything goes well; don't be frightened, it won't last.

Jules Renard

Blues is a chair, not a design for a chair or a better chair or a bigger chair. It is the first chair. It is a chair for sitting on, not for looking at or being appreciated. You sit on that music.

John Lennon

One never goes so far as when one doesn't know where one is going.

Johann Wolfgang von Goethe

If you keep a thing for seven years, you are sure to find a use for it.

Sir Walter Scott, *Woodstock*

All men know the utility of useful things,
but true wisdom lies in knowing the utility
of futility.

Chuang-tzu,
On Levelling All Things, c. 300 BC

Who's ever written the great work about
the immense effort required in order *not* to
create?

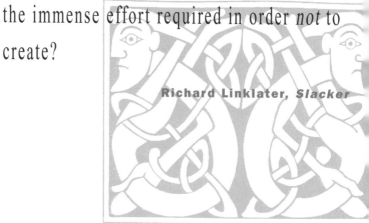

Richard Linklater, *Slacker*

What I aspired to be
And was not
Comforts me.

Robert Browning, *Rabbi Ben Ezra*

It takes character to withstand the rigors of
indolence.

Lord Thurlow in Alan Bennett's
The Madness of King George

Just take it a little easy, and we'll all get to
Grand Island in one piece.

Jack Kerouac, *On the Road*

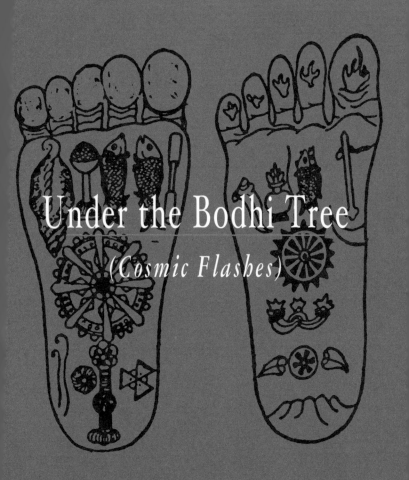

Under the Bodhi Tree

(Cosmic Flashes)

Bodhi Tree: n. (1) sacred wild fig under which the Buddha sat until he was more confused than ever; (2) an Egyptian queen? Ancient ruins? Nobody knows.

flash: (1) tr. v. to emerge suddenly in flame; (2) n. cosmic matter unexpectedly entering the mindstream while dowsing, dancing or milking the cow.

Australian mountain range: (1) not the site of Bob Dylan's 115th dream; (2) inhabited principally by wallabies and aborigines; (3) current abode of Owsley Stanley.

reincarnation: n. if you can't get it right this time around, you can always come back and screw things up again (see Buddha, above, for details).

Everyone is in the best seat.

John Cage

All thoughts of a turtle are turtle.

Ralph Waldo Emerson

Be crazy dumbsaint of the mind.

Jack Kerouac

The formula "Two and two make five" is not without its attractions.

Fyodor Dostoevsky,
Notes from Underground, 1864

The truth is silly putty.

Paul Krassner

Everybody's an artist. Everybody's God.

Yoko Ono

It's all the same fucking day, man.

Janis Joplin

Only useless things are indispensable.

Francis Picabia

Sometimes nothing can be a real cool hand.

Cool Hand Luke

The day is coming when a single carrot, freshly observed, will set off a revolution.

Paul Cézanne

The difference between false memories and true ones is the same as jewels: it is always the false ones that look the most real, the most brilliant.

Salvador Dali

Digressions, incontestably, are the sunshine.

Laurence Sterne,
Tristram Shandy

Superstition is the well of all truths.

Charles Baudelaire,
My Heart Laid Bare

There is no original truth, only original error.

Gaston Bachelard

An artist is his own fault.

John O'Hara

Miami Beach is where neon goes to die.

Lenny Bruce

Architecture will be soft and hairy.

Antonio Gaudí

Round numbers are always false.

James Boswell,
Life of Johnson

Everything tries to be round.

Black Elk Speaks

Money costs too much.

Ross McDonald,
The Goodbye Look

The basis of optimism is sheer terror.

Oscar Wilde

Somebody got lucky but it was an accident.

Bob Dylan

I've developed a new philosophy . . . I only dread one day at a time.

Charlie Brown

Take eloquence and wring its neck!

Paul Verlaine

The more things a man is ashamed of, the more respectable he is.

George Bernard Shaw, *Man and Superman*

Things are more like they are now than
they have ever been before.

I is another.

A-wop-bop-a-lula-a-wop-bam-boom!

Little Richard

It's the truth, even if it didn't happen.

Ken Kesey,
w Over the Cuckoo's Nest

...thing definite a man
renounces everything else.

George Santayana

What other people think of me is not my
business.

Andrew Kudlacik

I hate the sun but it's nice to know it's there.

Johnny Rotten

It's hard to bullshit the ocean. It's not listening, you know what I mean.

David Crosby

The gods love the obscure and hate the obvious.

The Upanishads,
800-500 BC

Plug in, freak out, fall down.

The Grateful Dead's response to Timothy Leary's "Tune in, turn on, drop out"

May you live all the days of your life.

Jonathan Swift

It'd be nice to publish alternate universes.

Jerry Garcia

This is my prediction for the future,
whatever hasn't happened *will* happen.

Religion, oh, just anoth
popularize art.

Ludwig Wittgenstein

Superstition brings bad luck.

Dr. Saul Gorn,
Compendium of Rarely Used Clichés

Confusion is mightier than the sword.

Abbie Hoffman

If I called the wrong number, why did you answer the phone?

James Thurber

My Way

(I'm a Solipsist. Isn't Everybody?)

solipsism: n. appealing theory that the self is the only reality (especially popular among philosophers and potheads).

my way: tr. v. (1) ignore the advice of others; (2) throw the I Ching until you get the answer you're looking for; (3) lie to your shrink; (4) remember: you are God, they are fools.

ego pogo: (1) confusion of the self with this sentence; (2) the hearing of ancient voices; (3) obeying unreasonable orders from dogs as in Son of Sam; (4) something to do with the right and left sides of the brain but I can't remember what.

Flaubert gave instructions to his servant to speak to him only on Sundays, and then only in order to say: "Sir, it is Sunday."

The Goncourt Journal

He was always late on principle, the principle being that punctuality is the thief of time.

Oscar Wilde, *The Picture of Dorian Gray*

I cling to my imperfection, as the very
essence of my being.

Anatole France,
The Garden of Epicurus, 1894

I've been on a calendar, but never on time.

Marilyn Monroe

I know who I was when I got up this morning, but I must have changed several times
since then.

Lewis Carroll,
Alice in Wonderland

Nobody can be exactly like me. Sometimes even I have trouble doing it.

Tallulah Bankhead

One's real life is so often the life that one does not lead.

Oscar Wilde

On my gravestone, I want to say "I told you I was sick." Achievement is for senators and scholars. At one time I had ambitions but I had them removed by a doctor in Buffalo.

Tom Waits

The radio doesn't like anybody but me
listening to it.

Taylor Mead,
On Amphetamine and in Europe

Anything awful makes me laugh.
I misbehaved once at a funeral.

Charles Lamb,
Letter to Southey, 1815

Thank heavens the sun has gone in, and
I don't have to go out and enjoy it.

Logan Pearsall Smith,
Afterthoughts

Leave me alone. I'm a lineman. I want to
be obscure.

Dennis Nelson,
Sports Illustrated

I am always at a loss how much to believe
my own stories.

Washington Irving,
Tales of a Traveler, 1824

When choosing between two evils I always take the one I've never tried before.

Mae West, *Klondike Annie*

Show my head to the people, it is worth seeing.

Georges Jacques Danton, last words, addressed to the executioner

(Sigh!) No weed in a *month!* I guess I might as well accept that athletic scholarship to Notre Dame and study business economics, after all!

Gilbert Shelton, *The Fabulous Furry Freak Brothers*

Anyone who paints a sky green and pastures blue ought to be sterilized.

Adolph Hitler

Hey! You! Get offa my cloud.

Mick Jagger/Keith Richards

I love Mickey Mouse more than any woman I've ever known.

Walt Disney

Why shave, when I can't think of a reason for living?

Jack Smith

I smash guitars because I like them.

Pete Townshend

I was much too far out all my life
And not waving but drowning.

Stevie Smith

No one should drive a hard bargain with
an artist.

Ludwig van Beethoven

Machines have less problems. I'd like to be a machine.

Andy Warhol

If only I had known I should have become a watchmaker.

Albert Einstein

Yes — around Concord.

**Henry David Thoreau,
on being asked if he travelled**

43 ➤

I don't care what is written about me as long as it isn't true.

Katharine Hepburn

If I didn't start painting, I would have raised chickens.

Grandma Moses

My life has been one long descent into respectability.

Mandy Rice Davies
[Profumo scandal]

The whole world is about three drinks
behind.

Humphrey Bogart

1) Write "I Love Paul" at the top of my
diary in my most perfect handwriting;
2) Listen to a Beatles record before sleep.
No other sound could assault my eardrums
after the *sacred* sound. If the dog barked,
I had to climb out of bed and start over.
In addition, I had to write his name down
every time I farted.

Pamela Des Barres,
I'm With the Band

Stay in your own movie.

Ken Kesey

There is less in this than meets the eye.

Tallulah Bankhead

Do I contradict myself?
Very well then I contradict myself.

Walt Whitman

To shine —

and to hell with everything else!

That is my motto —

and the sun's!

Vladimir Mayakovsky

"What do people catch in the Queensborough Bridge — bugs?" asked Wilbur.

"No," said Charlotte. "They don't catch anything. They just keep trotting back and forth across the bridge thinking there is something better on the other side. If they'd hang head-down at the top of the thing and wait quietly, maybe something good would come along. But no — with men it's rush, rush, rush every minute. I'm glad I'm a sedentary spider."

E.B. White,
Charlotte's Web

In the Waiting Room

(Family, Growing Up, Rules)

family: n. a bunch of annoying people who claim to be related to you.

family unit: considered sacred; seen as real cause of most foreign wars (along with religion, property and kitchen appliances).

grown up: n. (1) stage of life in which one forgets how to play with toys; (2) the ability to drink, smoke and, eventually, kill yourself.

youth: n. always use with one of the following clichés: "goes by too quickly" or ""wasted on the young."

rules: pl. n. (1) unreasonable advice from someone larger than yourself; (2) to be applied only to other people; (3) best to make them up as you go along; (4) exceptions always prove them.

This was all that passed between them on the subject, but henceforth Wendy knew that she must grow up. You always know after you are two. Two is the beginning of the end.

J.M. Barrie, *Peter Pan*

Stand firm in your refusal to remain conscious during algebra. In real life, I assure you, there is no such thing as algebra.

Fran Lebowitz

Parents are sometimes a bit of a disappointment to their children. They don't fulfill the promise of their early years.

Anthony Powell,
Dance to the Music of Time

He that hath no fools, knaves or beggars in his family was begot by a flash of lightning.

Thomas Fuller,
Gnomologia, 1732

If you cannot get rid of the family skeleton, you may as well make it dance.

George Bernard Shaw

All children are essentially criminal.

Denis Diderot, 1713-1784

There is the greatest practical benefit in making a few failures early in life.

Thomas Henry Huxley

If parents only realized how they bore their children!

Being born is like being kidnapped and sold into slavery.

The lullaby is the spell whereby the mother attempts to transform herself back from an ogre to a saint.

Thou has most tortuously corrupted the youth of the realm in erecting a grammar school.

William Shakespeare, *Henry VI*

Prizes bring bad luck. Academic prizes, prizes for virtue, decorations, all those inventions of the devil encourage hypocrisy and freeze the spontaneous upsurge of a free heart.

Charles Baudelaire

What is time? If you don't ask me, I know; but if you ask me, I don't know.

St. Augustine

A child of *five* would understand this. Send somebody to fetch a child of five!

Groucho Marx, *Duck Soup*

We are the people our parents warned us against.

Youth Movement Slogan, c. 1965

I am a student. Please do not fold, spindle
or mutilate me.

Free Speech Slogan, 1964

The most common error made with ducks
is trying to raise them like chickens.
Every type of bird must be managed
somewhat differently.

Raising the Home Duck Flock

Remember that as a teenager you are at the last stage in your life when you will be happy to hear the phone is for you.

Fran Lebowitz

No good deed will go unpunished.

Clare Booth Luce

In the first place God made idiots. That was for practice. Then he made school boards.

Mark Twain, *Following the Equator*

I wouldn't turn out the way I did if I didn't
have all the old-fashioned values to rebel
against.

Madonna

Improvement makes strait roads; but the
crooked roads without Improvement are the
roads of Genius.

William Blake,
The Marriage of Heaven and Hell

Banish wisdom, discard knowledge, and
gangsters will stop!

Chuang-tzu,
On Levelling All Things, c. 300 BC

The dawn of knowledge is usually the false
dawn.

Bernard De Voto,
The Course of Empire

.

No one is more liable to make mistakes than the man who acts only on reflection.

Marquis de Vauvenargues,
Reflections and Maxims, 1746

You never know what is enough unless you know what is more than enough.

William Blake,
The Marriage of Heaven and Hell

The end of all learning is recovery of the lost mind.

Mencius, c. 382-301 BC

There's nothing nobler than to put up with a few inconveniences like snakes and dust for the sake of absolute freedom.

Jack Kerouac,
Lonesome Traveller

The water was all slippy-sloppy in the larder and back passage. But Mr. Jeremy Fisher liked getting his feet wet; nobody ever scolded him, and he never caught a cold.

Beatrix Potter,
The Tale of Mr. Jeremy Fisher

Altered States
(Love, Magic, Drugs, Art and Otherness)

altered state: n. (1) not a country; (2) holding onto the grass so you don't fall *up*; (3) any situation in which you find yourself requiring a passport, a condom, tarot cards or a sugar cube; (4) any condition in which the phrase "colorless green ideas sleep furiously" makes sense to you; (5) the way we were.

reality: n. (1) a concept with which to threaten children; (2) considered unstable ever since Heisenberg's discovery of the Uncertainty Principle.

magic: n. (1) technique used to liquefy reality; (2) something that is always afoot.

"One can't believe impossible things."

"I daresay you haven't had much practice," said the Queen. "When I was your age I always did it for one half an hour a day. Why, sometimes I believed as many as six impossible things before breakfast."

Lewis Carroll,
Through the Looking Glass

I do not take drugs, I am drugs.

Salvador Dali

A generation that lives with no purpose and
aim is a generation that lives in ecstasy.

Jonas Mekas

I drink to make other people interesting.

George Jean Nathan

the thing about opium
dens is everyone minds his
own business.

Taylor Mead,
On Amphetamine and in Europe

Grass sits you down on your fanny. You can't do anything but see things.

Joni Mitchell

When one wants to get rid of an insupportable pressure, one needs hashish.

Friedrich Nietzsche

The pilgrims found a hallucinogenic world in America when they came and destroyed it. Now the drugs will bring it back again. They will give us back a world with no separation between past, present and future. They will gives us back reality.

Conrad Brooks

I didn't really want to enjoy the moment. I wanted to take drugs.

Doug Fleger,
member of the Knack

I found psychedelics to be keys to worlds
that have always existed. The kaleidoscopic
pictures that one experiences under, say,
mescaline, aren't concealed in the white
crystals inside the gelatine capsule.
They are always in the mind. In the world.
Already. The chemical allows the picture
to be seen.

Ken Kesey, *On the Bus*

I habituated myself to simple hallucination:
I saw a mosque where there was a factory,
a school of drummers made up of angels,
carriages on the roads of heaven.

Arthur Rimbaud

If smoking dope doesn't damage your
brain, why do so many Jamaicans believe
a dead Ethiopian is god?

Darius James

Versailles, for one who has taken hashish,
is not too large, or eternity too long.

Walter Benjamin

In dreams the things I see, see me just as much as I see them.

Paul Valery, *Analecta*

Fifteen apparitions have I seen;
The worst a coat upon a coat-hanger.

W.B. Yeats,
The Apparitions

I'm very high now.

attributed to Lenny Bruce by a medium
after his death (in Paul Krassner's
Ravings of an Unconfined Nut)

Nothing great is achieved without
chimeras.

Ernest Renan,
L'Avenir de la Science, 1890

Pot will probably be legal in ten years.
Why? Because in this audience
probably every other one of you knows a
law student who smokes pot, who will
become a senator, who will legalize it to
protect himself. But then no one will
smoke it anymore. You'll see.

Lenny Bruce

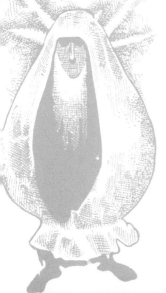

A hundred doses of happiness is not enough. Send to the drugstore for another bottle, and when that is finished for another.

Aldous Huxley

No human being, however great, or powerful, was ever so free as a fish.

John Ruskin, *The Two Paths,* **1859**

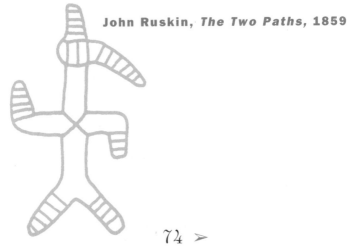

"Look, sir," answered Sancho Panza, "those which appear yonder are not giants, but windmills; and what seem to be arms are the sails, which whirled about by the wind, make the millstone go."

"It is very evident," answered Don Quixote, "that thou art not versed in the business of adventures."

Miguel de Cervantes,
Don Quixote

The TV set was black and white, but LBJ on LSD was purple and orange.

Paul Krassner

The closer one looks at a word, the greater the distance from which it looks back.

Karl Kraus,
Pro domo et mundo

They'll never legalize marijuana because no one can find the petition.

I feel that any form of psychotherapy is strongly contraindicated for addicts.

William Burroughs

Reality is just a crutch for people who can't deal with drugs.

Lily Tomlin

I will go and see whether there is a rat
in the rat-trap, we could make a coachman
of him.

Cinderella

You have merely painted what is! Anyone
can paint what is; the real secret is to paint
what isn't.

Oscar Mandel,
Chi Po and the Sorcerer

The moon is a monk who gazes enviously at the earth, or a cat who walks on a rug of stars.

Friedrich Nietzsche

White magic is poetry; black magic is anything that actually works.

Victor Anderson
(Priest of the Faery Tradition)

Oh, what a blow that phantom dealt me!

Miguel de Cervantes,
Don Quixote

If you go expressly to look at the moon, it becomes tinsel.

Ralph Waldo Emerson

When it snows during the night you can tell something is different, even before you open your eyes.

Reginald & Galdys Laubin,
The Indian Tipi

Space no longer exists: the street pavement, soaked by rain beneath the glare of electric lamps, becomes immensely deep and gapes to the center of the earth.

Balla, Boccioni, et al.,
Futurist Paintings Technical Manifesto

Oh, that I now cou'd by some Chymic Art
To Sperm convert my Vitals and my Heart,
That at one Thrust I might my Soul translate,
And in the Womb myself regenerate; There
steep'd in Lust, nine Months I would remain
Then boldly fuck my passage out again.

John Wilmot, Earl of Rochester
"The Wish," 1678

To avoid abject stupidity a man must always
be a little mad.

Michel de Montaigne
Essays, 1580

The road of excess leads to the palace of
wisdom.

William Blake,
The Marriage of Heaven and Hell

I became insane . . . with intervals of
horrible sanity.

Edgar Allan Poe

The words–*are* they words?–are sweating,
liquefying back into the images from which
they came . . . shotgun shacks, live oaks,
gris-gris conjure women with yellow teeth,
rotting porches, bo weevils, demon-haunted
crossroads, rootless, horse-mad heroes
popping up *between* the words.

David Dalton and Rock Scully,
Living with the Dead

We want to enclose the universe in a work
of art. Individual objects do not exist
any more.

Gino Severini,
Futurist Manifesto, 1913

Human kind
Cannot bear much reality.

T.S. Eliot, *Four Quartets*

"Hello, Rabbit," he said. "Is that you?"
"Let's pretend it isn't," said Rabbit, "and see what happens."

A.A. Milne,
Winnie the Pooh

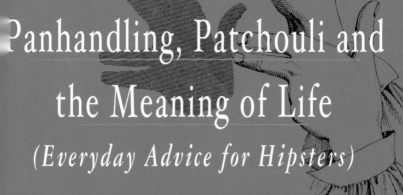

Panhandling, Patchouli and the Meaning of Life

(Everyday Advice for Hipsters)

advice: n. (1) an unsolicited opinion from one not in a position to give it; (2) best ignored if you want to find your true nature.

hipster: n. (1) indispensable addition to any party; (2) anyone who wears shades, especially at night; (3) connoisseur of crash pads and the vibe (see below).

vibe: n. (1) essential to tune in to; (2) comes in only two forms — good or bad; (3) similar to aura but faster; (4) irrational assumption based on any tingling sensation.

Whenever you receive a letter from a creditor write fifty lines upon some extra-terrestrial subject and you will be saved.

Charles Baudelaire, *Squibs*

Every revolutionary needs a color TV.

Jerry Rubin

Mistrust first impulses. They are always good.

Charles de Talleyrand, 1754-1838

What's wrong with dropping out? To me,
this is the whole point: one's right to
withdraw from a social environment that
offers no spiritual sustenance, and to *mind
one's own business.*

William Burroughs

The only way to be sure of catching a train
is to miss the one before it.

G.K. Chesterton

The first prerogative of an artist in any medium is to make a fool of himself.

Pauline Kael

SURFACE AT ONCE. THE SHIP IS SINKING.

Marshall McLuhan

He who asks fortunetellers the future unwittingly forfeits an inner intuition of coming events that is a thousand times more exact than anything they may say.

Walter Benjamin

Never play cards with a man called *Doc*. Never eat in a place called *Mom's*. Never sleep with a woman whose troubles are worse than your own.

Nelson Algren

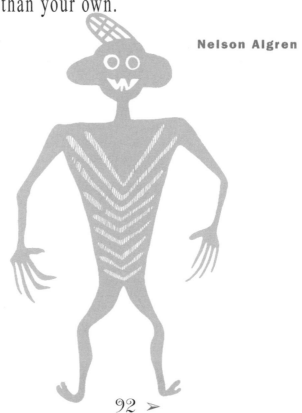

The best way to do is to be.

Lao Tzu

To do is to be.

Friedrich Nietzsche

To be is to do.

Emanuel Kant

Do be do be do.

Frank Sinatra

In love, as in nearly all human affairs, a satisfactory relationship is the result of a misunderstanding.

Charles Baudelaire,
My Heart Laid Bare

If you don't like what you're doing, you can always pick up your needle and move to another groove.

Timothy Leary

Cheer up, the worst is yet to come.

Philander Chase Johnson,
"Shooting Stars"

Think sideways!

Edward De Bono

Mistakes are almost always of a sacred nature. Never try to correct them.

Salvador Dali,
Diary of a Mad Genius

Nothing is so perfectly amusing as a total change of ideas.

Laurence Sterne,
Tristram Shandy

Row, row, row your boat
Gently down the stream
Merrily, merrily, merrily
Life is but a dream

Traditional

Forget the Buddha! Sit under the Bodhi
tree any time you like.

Toby Dalton

Let us beware of common-sense, inspira-
tion and evidence.

Charles Baudelaire,
My Heart Laid Bare

Chi Wen Tzu always thought three times before taking action. Twice would have been quite enough.

Confucius,
Analects, 5th century BC

If your morals make you dreary, depend upon it, they are wrong.

Robert Louis Stevenson

There is also a time to throw aside discretion and among fools to play the fool.

Menander, 342-292 BC

Stuckness shouldn't be avoided. It's the
psychic precursor of all real understanding.

Robert M. Pirsig,
Zen and the Art of Motorcycle Maintenance

Pay close attention to what's going on in
your mind and everything will be better.

Ed Balchowsky

If I'd observed all the rules, I'd never
have got any where.

Marilyn Monroe

Get out of the way of Justice. She is blind.

Stanislaw Jerzy Lec,
More Unkempt Thoughts

Never contend with a man who had nothing
to lose.

Baltazar Gracián,
The Art of Worldly Wisdom, 1647

If a man once indulges himself in murder, very soon he comes to think little of robbing; and from robbing he comes next to drinking and Sabbath-breaking, and from that to incivility and procrastination.

Thomas De Quincey,
Murder Considered as One of the Fine Arts, 1827

Of the 36 alternatives, running away is best.

Chinese Proverb

100 ➤

When you arise in the morning, you should do last night's dirty dishes . . . then you should sing a simple melody (of your own choice) . . . then you should call somebody up (not me) . . . then go to the store . . . buy some asparagus! Then meet a new person, go home, take LSD, say a prayer, breathe ten times, stand on your head, set your watch, take a shit and pick your nose. . . .

R. Crumb, *Mr. Natural*

Buy goo.

2nd Avenue subway graffiti

The United States

of Amnesia

Or How I Learned to Stop Worrying

and Love the Bomb)

America: bomb shelters, Fourth of July, missile silos, baseball, English as a second language, Japanese cars, high school confidential, Hallmark cards, teachers' dirty looks, bermudas, barbeques, Bugs Bunny, this book, commercials, malls, cineplexes, Fluffernutter, demolition derbies, rednecks, drug czars, Disneyworld, crack, washerdryers, grits, drive-ins, Velveeta, James Brown, blues and what's so funny about peace, love and understanding?

the sixties: vibes, hobbits, hexagrams, head shops, gods-eyes, grooving, geodesic domes, tie-dyed t-shirts, "far out," feedback, flashbacks, patchouli oil, brown rice, green plastic Ravi Shankar LPs, tarot cards, sinsimilla, auras, crabs, paisley, panhandling, ying yang, lava lamps, Zig-zag papers, FM radio, peace signs, the underground press, black light, crash pads, rock festivals, hare Krishna, tripping, tepees, joss sticks, LSD, DMT, MDA, MMDA, Mu, Atlantis and the Grateful Dead.

We have nothing to fear but sanity itself.

**Robin Williams,
*Mork & Mindy***

Another victory like that and we're
done for!

**Pyrrhus,
*Plutarch's Lives***

America, we love you as the child loves
the father who sits slobbering in his corner
eating flies and spiders.

Paul Kantner

Anything anybody can say about America is true.

Up on the Madison Fork, the *Wasiches* had found much of the yellow metal that they worship and that makes them crazy.

God looks after fools, drunks and the United States.

We have met the enemy and he is us.

Pogo

All kings is mostly rapscallions.

Mark Twain,
The Adventures of Huckleberry Finn

Believe me, that was a happy age, before the days of architects, before the days of builders.

Senecca,
Epistle 90, 5 BC-65 AD

Don Quixote is the true American . . . you
do not have to look in many American eyes
to suddenly meet somewhere the beautiful
grave lunacy of his gaze.

Tennessee Williams

Any smoothly functioning technology will
have the appearance of magic.

Arthur C. Clarke

America is the only nation in history which miraculously has gone directly from barbarism to degeneration without the usual interval of civilization.

Georges Clemenceau

The youth of America is their oldest tradition. It has been going on for 300 years.

Oscar Wilde,
A Woman of No Importance

Peace on earth by any means necessary.

'60s saying

109 ➤

Abomunists demand the re-establishment of
the government in its rightful home at
Disneyland.

Bob Kaufman,
The Abomunist Manifesto

I saw the bathroom fixtures as a kind of
American Trinity.

Claes Oldenburg

America is a mistake! A giant mistake!

Sigmund Freud

Fools! Assholes! Devout Citizens! Stop it!
Go home to your radios!

LeRoi Jones/Amiri Baraka

Beware of leaders, heroes, organizers.
Watch that stuff. Beware of structure
freaks. They do not understand. We know
the system doesn't work because we're
living in the ruins.

Chester Anderson

That so few now dare to be eccentric marks
the chief danger of our time.

John Stuart Mill

If a man were permitted to make all the
ballads, he should not care who should
make the laws of a nation.

Andrew Fletcher of Saltun, 1704

Those who would take over the earth
And shape it to their will
Never, I notice, succeed.

Lao Tzu, *The Way of Life*

It is difficult *not* to write satire.

Juvenal, *Satires*, 60 BC

If one man leads
Another must follow
How silly that is
And how false!

Lao Tzu, *The Way of Life*

The worst of doing one's duty was that it apparently unfitted one for doing anything else.

Edith Wharton,
The Age of Innocence

Puritanism — the haunting fear that someone, somewhere may be happy.

H.L. Mencken

Of course, don't ever tell anybody that they're *not* free, 'cause they're gonna get real busy killin' and maimin' to prove that they are.

Easy Rider

Life is like Sanskirt read to a pony.

Lou Reed

One has to multiply thoughts to the point
where there aren't enough policemen to
control them.

Stanislaw Jerzy Lec,
Unkempt Thoughts

"Sho! They *got* to have it against the law!
Shoot everybody get high. Wouldn't be
anybody get up and feed the chickens, hee,
hee."

Terry Southern,
"Red Dirt Marijuana"

Scandal begins when the police put a stop to it.

Karl Kraus

Rock 'n' roll is a way of life — meaning acid, Woodstock, the Maharishi and police brutality.

Pete Townshend

Maggie's Farm
(The Day Gig)

Maggie's Farm: Bob Dylan no longer works there.

the day gig: by and by all those things that once troubled me took on a fuzzy, surrealistic glow—subway tokens, time clocks, the water cooler, non-dairy creamer, in & out boxes, pay checks, garnishees, downsizing, pink slips and trolls with cute little sayings on them.

It was such a lovely day I thought it was a pity to get up.

W. Somerset Maugham

Oh thrice and four times happy those who plant cabbages!

Rabelais,
Gargantua and Pantagruel, 1532

I feel closest to Hell when I'm thinking about money.

Pharoah Sanders

It is not real work unless you would rather be doing something else.

J.M. Barrie

To be a useful person has always appeared to me to be something quite horrible.

Charles Baudelaire,
My Heart Laid Bare

If a thing is worth doing it is worth doing badly.

G.K. Chesterton

Anyone can do any amount of work,
provided it isn't the work he's supposed
to be doing.

Robert Benchley

Beware all enterprises that require new
clothes.

Henry David Thoreau,
Walden

Monkeys very sensibly refrain from speech,
lest they should be set to earn their livings.

Kenneth Grahame,
The Golden Age

The only thing that keeps half the people alive in factories is the fucking radio on all day.

Johnny Rotten

I wanted to be a singer because I didn't want to sweat.

Elvis Presley

I'd rather read, tell stories, crack jokes, talk, laugh — anything but work.

Abraham Lincoln

Perpetual devotion to what a man calls his business is only to be sustained by perpetual neglect of many other things.

Robert Louis Stevenson

Work with some men is as besetting a sin as idleness.

Samuel Butler

In the yearly statistics of suicides, why don't we count lovers who get married, poets who take a seat in the Chamber of Deputies or the Senate, young wits who go into journalism?

Henry Murger

Objection, evasion, happy distrust, pleasure in mockery are signs of health: everything absolute belongs in pathology.

Friedrich Nietzsche

Just because you have a computer, doesn't mean you can't be stupid.

Beavis & Butthead

Work is the refuge of people who have nothing better to do.

Oscar Wilde

If not from inclination at least from despair, as I have proved, to work is less wearisome than to amuse oneself.

Charles Baudelaire,
My Heart Laid Bare

It is wonderful when a calculation is made,
how little the mind is actually employed in
the discharge of any profession.

Samuel Johnson

It's true that hard work never killed
anybody, but I figure, why take the chance?

Ronald Reagan

Ouroboros

(Eternal Questions About Life,
Death, God and Cabbages)

ouroboros: n. (1) Alchemical snake that bites its own tail; (2) the beginning is in the end and the end is in the beginning: (3) serpentine philosophy as outlined by Jerry Garcia on *Playboy After Dark*.

god: n. any virtuoso guitar player.

eternal questions: Who wrote the book of love? Can't you hear me knockin'? What's goin' on? How high the moon? Where did our love go? Who calls the English teacher Daddy-o? And have you seen your mother, baby, standing in the shadow?

One world at a time!

Henry David Thoreau,
on being asked his opinion of the hereafter

Who are those who will eventually be
damned. Oh the others, the others,
the others!

The Roycroft Dictionary &
Book of Epigrams, 1923

Just superficial stuff like what happened to
you in your lifetime is nothing compared
to the container which holds all your
information.

Jerry Garcia

Chemistry is applied theology.

Owsley Stanley

The most merciful thing in the world is the inability of the human mind to correlate all its contents.

H.P. Lovecraft

I'm a worm, I'm God.

Johnny Rotten

Every day people are straying away from
the church and going back to God. Really.

Lenny Bruce

O senseless man, who could not
possibly make a worm, but will make
gods by dozens.

Michel de Montaigne,
Essays, 1580

Madame, all stories, if continued far
enough, end in death, and he is no true
storyteller who would keep that from you.

Ernest Hemingway,
Death in the Afternoon

It's just a kiss away.

Mick Jagger/Keith Richards

The opposite of a correct statement is a
false statement. But the opposite of profound truth may be another profound truth.

Niels Bohr

Instead of Messiahs we always had big
rock 'n' roll stars. We like to see who
we're worshipping.

Patti Smith

Back of the sun and way deep under our
feet, at the earth's center, are not a couple
of noble mysteries but a couple of joke
books.

Tennessee Williams

Don't be on the side of the angels, it's too lowering.

D.H. Lawrence

I think there are innumerable gods. What we on earth call God is a little tribal God who has made an awful mess.

William Burroughs

Saintliness is also a temptation.

Jean Anouilh,
Becket

I never pass by a wooden fetish, a gilded
Buddha, a Mexican idol without reflecting:
perhaps this is the true God.

Charles Baudelaire

Only he who is in the highest heaven
knows. Or perhaps he does not know!

Rig-Veda, **1700 BC**

I think, myself, that in 1903, we passed
through the remains of a powdered world —
left over from an ancient inter-planetary
dispute, brooding in space. . . .

Charles Fort

Explanation separates us from astonish-
ment, which is the only gateway to the
incomprehensible.

Eugène Ionesco,
Découvertes

Formlessness and chaos lead to new forms.
And new order. Closer to, probably, what
the real order is.

Jerry Garcia

All these melodramas, these roles, are merely garments of central casting, and anyone — the postman, the cop, the speed freak — can be Buddha.

Baba Ram Das

Truth is one, but error proliferates. Man tracks it down and cuts it up into little pieces hoping to turn it into grains of truth.

René Daumal,
The Life of the Truth

It is good to love the unknown.

Charles Lamb,
Valentine's Day

Immortality—a fate worse than death.

Edgar A. Shoaff

Old hippies don't die. They just lie low
until the laughter stops and their time
comes round again.

Joseph Gallivan

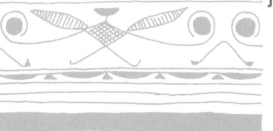

Posterity is just around the corner.

George S. Kaufman

I want death to find me planting my cabbages.

Michel de Montaigne,
Essays, 1580

I go to seek the Great Perhaps.

Rabelais, last words, 1553